Pollination

Dona Herweck Rice

Consultants

Sally Creel, Ed.D.
Curriculum Consultant

Leann Iacuone, M.A.T., NBCT, ATC
Riverside Unified School District

Image Credits: p.2 blickwinkel/Alamy; pp.10–11 (background), 18 (background) iStock; p.18 (top) Cheryl Power/Science Source; p.30 Scimat/Science Source; p.15 (bottom) GAP Photos/Getty Images; pp.28–29 (illustrations) Janelle Bell-Martin; all other images from Shutterstock.

Library of Congress Cataloging-in-Publication Data

Rice, Dona, author.
Pollination / Dona Herweck Rice ; consultant, Sally Creel, Ed.D., curriculum consultant, Leann Iacuone, M.A.T., NBCT, ATC Riverside Unified School District, Jill Tobin, California Teacher of the Year semi-finalist, Burbank Unified School District.
pages cm
Summary: "Living things depend on one another. Insects, water, and wind help plants grow new plants. They have an important role in nature. All these things work together to keep one another alive."
— Provided by publisher.
Audience: K to grade 3.
Includes index.
ISBN 978-1-4807-4598-8 (pbk.)
ISBN 978-1-4807-5065-4 (ebook)
1. Pollination—Juvenile literature.
2. Plants—Reproduction—Juvenile literature. I. Title.
QK926.R53 2015
581.3—dc23

2014014103

Teacher Created Materials
5301 Oceanus Drive
Huntington Beach, CA 92649-1030
http://www.tcmpub.com

ISBN 978-1-4807-4598-8

Printed by: 590835
Printed in: Taiwan

Table of Contents

Teamwork

Muscle and bone. Fish and water. Milk and cookies. Some of the best things in life **depend** on each other.

Well, milk and cookies may not depend on each other. But most plants and a lot of insects do! They need each other to **survive**.

Insects seek pollen in flowers. Some, like the Venus flytrap, trick the bugs and eat them!

New plants don't just decide to grow one day. They need help to get things started. That is where insects come in. Wind and water help, too. They make it possible for most plants to grow new plants.

A Big Job!

More than 90 percent of all plants need a **pollinator**.

Pollination

Insects, wind, and water help plants. They do this through pollination. That is how they carry **pollen** from plant to plant. This starts the process that allows new plants to grow.

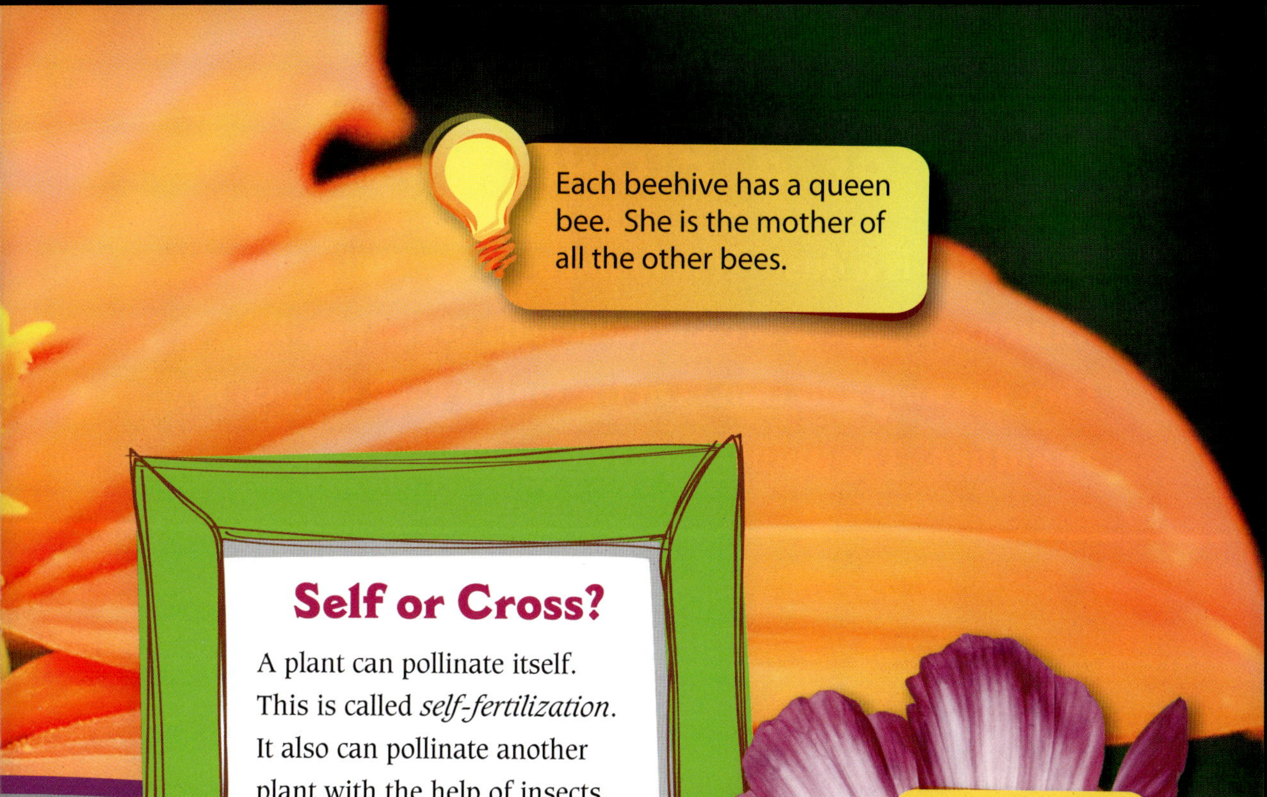

Each beehive has a queen bee. She is the mother of all the other bees.

Self or Cross?

A plant can pollinate itself. This is called *self-fertilization*. It also can pollinate another plant with the help of insects, animals, wind, or water. That's called *cross-fertilization*.

Parts of a Flower

Pollen is a dust. It is found at the end of a flower's **stamens.** Stamens are the male part of the plant. They are long and thin. On the end of each stamen is an **anther.** The anther holds the pollen.

Achoo!

Some people are allergic to pollen. When there is a lot of flower pollen, they may sneeze and sneeze and sneeze!

anther
stamen
The pollen is the
dust on the anther.

To make a new plant, the pollen must reach the **pistil**. The pistil is the female part of the plant. The **stigma** is at the top of the pistil. The tube below it is the **style**. The **ovary** is at the base of the pistil. This is where seeds are made.

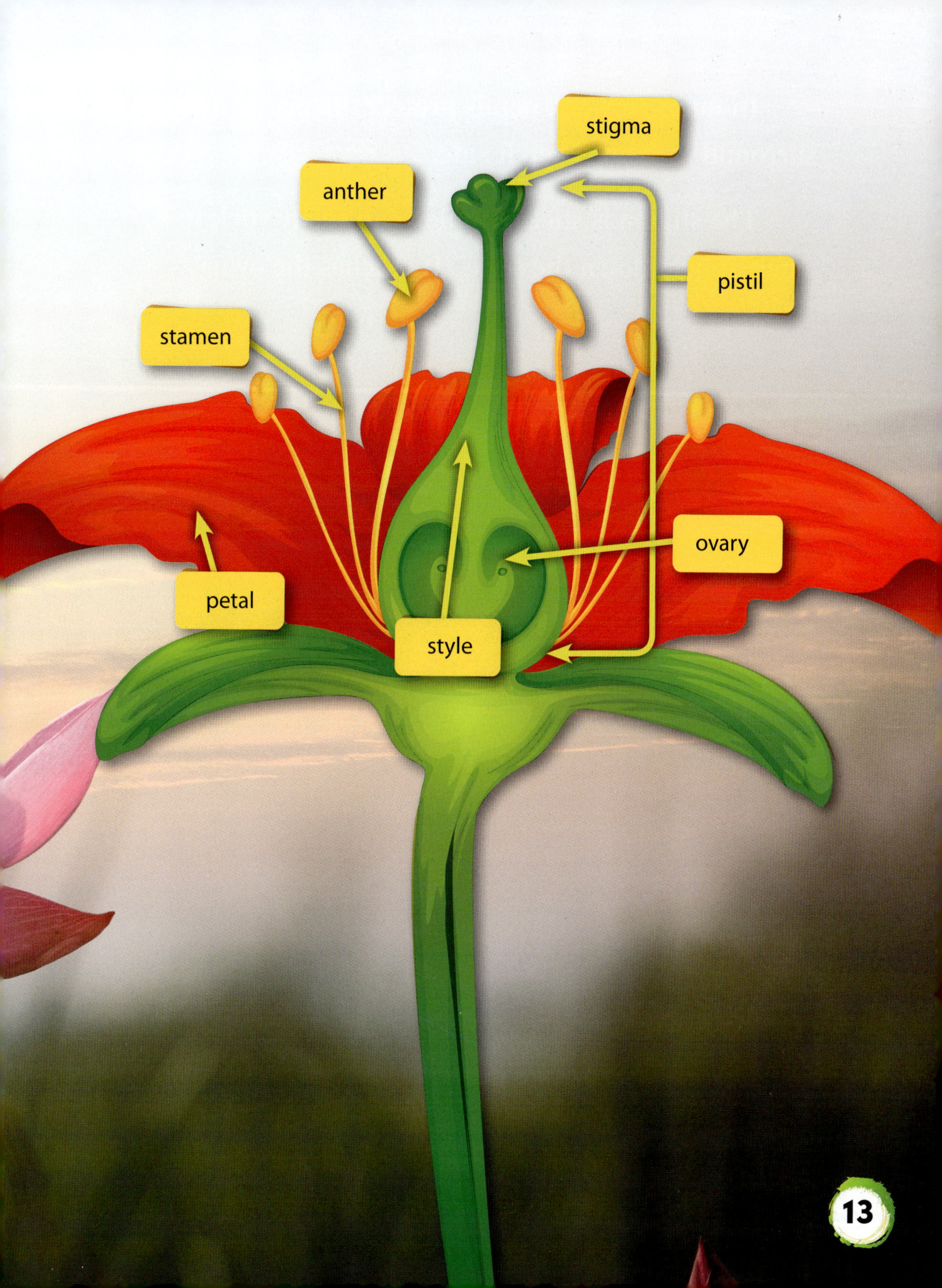
stigma
anther
pistil
stamen
ovary
petal
style

In many flowers, petals protect the pistil. They surround it. They keep it safe.

The stigma is sticky. Pollen can easily stick to it. Then, it goes down the style. It reaches the ovary.

Pistils may look different, but they all have the same purpose.

After cotton plants flower, they make tiny hairs. These hairs make the fabric we use for clothing.

One Plant or Two?

Some plants, such as corn, have separate male and female parts on the same plant. Other plants, such as willow trees, have male and female parts on different plants.

stamen on a willow tree

Help Is on the Way

Plants do not get up and move on their own. They have no way to move their pollen to make new plants. They need help. Insects, wind, and water give them the help they need.

Pollen can be carried on an animal's fur.

Pollen sticks to insects when they feed on flowers. They carry the pollen on them as they fly. Some of that pollen falls off. Or it can be caught by the wind or rain. Either way, the pollen's journey begins!

Pollen Grains

If you look at pollen through a microscope, this is what you will see. You can tell by its spiky shape that a pollen grain can stick to things easily.

Pollen sticks to a bee's body.

Corny

Corn has separate male and female flowers. Its stamens are the corn tassels. Its pistils are the ears of corn that have not yet developed.

Fertilize

In a plant, the male cell fertilizes the female cell. Pollen is the male cell. The female cells are held in the ovary. They make seeds together.

Pollinators

The helpers that carry the pollen are pollinators. Their job is important! Without them, there would be no new plants.

Bats, moths, and birds are also good pollinators.

Wind and water help a lot, too. But two types of living things are the biggest heroes. They are bees and butterflies.

Good for Them, Too!

By helping plants, bees and butterflies also help themselves. They feed from the flowers. They need new plants to keep growing!

Bees

Bees are some of the best pollinators! They have hairy bodies that trap pollen. They usually visit the same kind of flower. This keeps the pollen where it is needed. Their small size and short legs help bees get inside flowers, too.

Butterflies have taste buds on their feet. They also have a long tubelike tongue they use like a straw to suck up liquid.

Butterflies

Butterflies trap pollen on their bodies, too. They walk around on groups of flowers. This helps spread pollen.

Nature's Puzzle

Nature is like a puzzle. Each part of nature connects to make an amazing whole. Pollination is like that. Plants, insects, wind, and water are parts of the puzzle. And nature needs every piece!

Let's Do Science!

What is inside a flower? See for yourself!

What to Get

- butter knife
- flower with stamens and pistil

What to Do

1. Look at the flower. See how it is shaped. See all its parts.

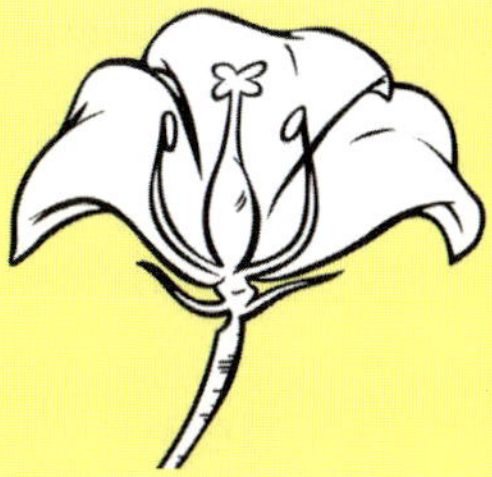

2. Have an adult help you find the stamens. Touch and study them. What do you notice?

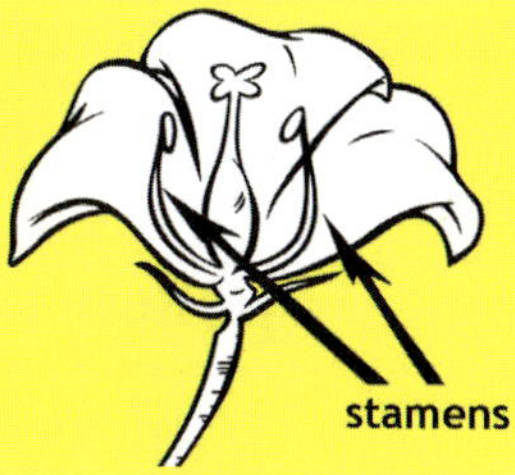

3. Have an adult help you find the pistil. Touch and study it. What do you notice?

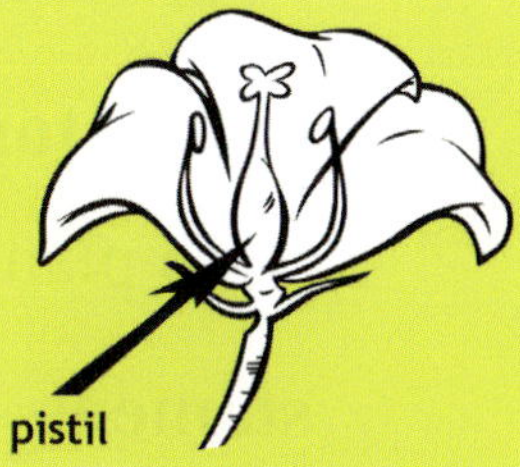

4. Carefully remove the pistil. Cut it open with an adult. What do you see?

5. Draw pictures of the parts of the flower. What do you think each part does?

Glossary

anther—the part of a flower that holds the pollen

depend—to count on or need

ovary—the part of a plant where seeds are made

pistil—the female part of a flower

pollen—dust made by plants and carried to other plants, usually by wind or insects, so that plants can produce seeds

pollinator—something that carries pollen from plant to plant

stamens—parts of a flower that make pollen

stigma—the top part in the center of a flower that receives the pollen

style—the long, thin center part of the pistil

survive—to remain alive

Index

Your Turn!

Create a Pollinator

Take a look at the world around you to find signs of pollinators. Then, use craft items or things from nature to make a model of a pollinator. What does the pollinator do to carry pollen? How can you show that?